Watch Out, There's a Ghost About!

Best Wishes,

Ian Blunt

Other poetry titles you might enjoy:

Watch Out, There's a Ghost About!

Creepy poems
collected by John Foster

OXFORD
UNIVERSITY PRESS

OXFORD
UNIVERSITY PRESS

Great Clarendon Street, Oxford OX2 6DP

Oxford University Press is a department of the University of Oxford.
It furthers the University's objective of excellence in research, scholarship,
and education by publishing worldwide in

Oxford New York

Auckland Bangkok Buenos Aires
Cape Town Chennai Dar es Salaam Delhi Hong Kong Istanbul
Karachi Kolkata Kuala Lumpur Madrid Melbourne Mexico City Mumbai
Nairobi São Paulo Shanghai Singapore Taipei Tokyo Toronto
with an associated company in Berlin

Oxford is a registered trade mark of Oxford University Press
in the UK and in certain other countries

British Library Cataloguing in Publication Data available

ISBN 0-19-276278-8

1 3 5 7 9 10 8 6 4 2

Typeset by Mary Tudge (Typesetting Services)

Printed in the UK by Cox & Wyman Ltd, Reading, Berkshire

Cover illustration by Ellis Nadler

Inside illustrations by Chris Mould

Contents

Watch Out, There's a Ghost About!

Watch out, there's a ghost about,
Tall as the tallest tree.
Watch out, there's a ghost about,
That can shrink to the size of a flea.

Watch out, there's a ghost about,
Playing chase with the wind.
Watch out, there's a ghost about,
And all it wants is a friend.

Watch out, there's a ghost about,
Sliding under the door.
Watch out, there's a ghost about,
Creeping across the floor.

Watch out, there's a ghost about,
Hovering behind your chair.
Watch out, there's a ghost about,
Combing cold hands through your hair.

Watch out, there's a ghost about,
And it's getting bolder.
Watch out, there's a ghost about,
Sitting on your shoulder . . .

Kevin McCann

The Family Spook

I am a werewolf
With fangs sharp and white
I howl at the moon
And I hunt folk at night.

My father's a vampire
Who sleeps in a casket
He likes to drink blood
And keeps bats in a basket.

My mother's a witch
Who cackles and moans
She casts nasty spells
And she boils up men's bones.

My sister Matilda's
A ghost with no head
She rattles her chains
At the foot of your bed.

Together we frighten
We shock and we scare
We're the Family Spook
And we'll find you. BEWARE!

Richard Caley

Listen

When the landing light goes out
And the stars begin to glitter,
Did you hear that distant shout
Or that secret patter-pitter?

Hold your breath and lie quite still,
Let the darkness slowly settle . . .
What was that—the creak of wood?
What was that—the clink of metal?

Or the trees that sway outside
In the wind, their dry leaves rustling?
Or could it be that night's dark cloak
Softly hides a ghostly bustling?

And up there beyond the ceiling
Did you catch a sudden squeak—
And suspect that in a moment
There'll erupt a long high *SHRIEK!!*

And a gurgling and a splatter
And a bubbling and a plop,
And that through the lath and plaster
Something horrible will drop . . . ?

But don't worry, so you say,
For it's all inside my head . . .
Until you hear that dragging noise
From underneath the bed!

Steve Bowkett

Counting Steps

Going down
to breakfast
I counted
thirteen steps
on the stairs.

Coming up
to bed
I counted
fourteen steps.

Now I'm in bed
and worried.
Where did
the extra step
come from?

Everyone is asleep.
I creep on to the landing.
I count the steps again.

Twelve.

Roger Stevens

The Grebs

When at night in bed I sleep
I hear the grebs around me creep,
I hear their whiskers scrape the floor,
I hear their fingers at the door.

I see their eyes shine in the dark,
I hear them squeal, I hear them bark.
'Oh, Grebs, if you'll just go away,
I'll be good tomorrow, all day!'

But voices say, 'Too late, too late!
We want you, dead or alive!'
I tremble, shiver, shake and quiver,
And beneath the bedclothes hide.

And feet and whiskers round me run
And closer, closer, closer come . . .
'Oh, Grebs, if you'll just go away,
I'll be good tomorrow, all day!'

Too late,
Too late,
We're here . . .

Mike Harding

What's That?

What's that rustling at the window?
Only the curtains flapping in the breeze.

What's that groaning in the garden?
Only the branches swaying in the trees.

What's that rattling at the front door?
Only the wind in the letter-box flap.

What's that drumming in the bathroom?
Only the dripping of the leaking tap.

What's that hissing in the front room?
Only the gas as it burns in the fire.

What's that murmur in the kitchen?
Only the whirring of the tumble dryer.

What's that shadow lurking
    in the corner beside the door?
It's only your clothes where you left them
    lying on the bedroom floor.

John Foster

The Ghost in the Washing Machine

A ghost is stuck in our washing machine,
And I say serve him right.
He got mixed up with the sheets, you see,
And now he's whiter than white.

His eyes are staring, he's really glaring,
He's not enjoying the ride.
I'll set him free at half past three
As soon as he's tumble-dried.

Kaye Umansky

The Lurkers

On our Estate
When it's getting late
In the middle of the night
They come in flocks
From beneath tower-blocks
And crawl towards the light

Down the Crescent
Up the Drive
Late at night
They come alive
Lurking here and lurking there
Sniffing at the midnight air

Up the Shopping Centre
You might just hear their call
Something like a bin-bag
Moving by the wall

Lurking at the bus-stop
Seen through broken glass
Something dark and slimy
Down the underpass

On our Estate
When it's getting late
In the middle of the night
There are things that lurk
About their work
Till dawn puts them to flight.

Adrian Henri

The Alleyway

The alleyway is crooked,
The alleyway is damp,
The alleyway has corners,
Untouched by any lamp,
The alleyway has bats in
And ghosts and thieves and rats in,
So please don't make me
Please don't make me
Please don't make me
Please don't make me
Please don't make me walk the alleyway.

The alleyway is dirty,
The alleyway is mean,
You see things in the alleyway
You wish you'd never seen,
The alleyway has litter
And smells and broken glass,
And things like rags that flap to catch
Your ankles as you pass,
And slimy stuff you tread in
And everything I dread in,
So please don't make me
Please don't make me
Please don't make me
Please don't make me
Please don't make me
Please don't make me walk the alleyway.

Richard Edwards

Mr Alucard

Down our street there's someone new
Living next to the churchyard:
He is a man of mystery
Called Mr Alucard.
That's a strange name for starters,
But there's more that mystifies:
His wolfish grin, his sharp white teeth,
His very piercing eyes.
Wrapped in a big, black, batlike cloak
He goes out late at night
And I swear he casts no shadow
As he passes the street light.
Yesterday he said to me,
'What a lovely throat you've got,'
And he stared and smiled a secret smile;
It worries me a lot.
There's something odd about his name . . .
I can't think what it is,
And I'd like to make some sense
Of those weird ways of his.
I definitely need some help,
So please try very hard
To help me solve the mystery
Of Mr Alucard.

Eric Finney

Count Dracula

Count Dracula
At blood-sports is quite spectacular.
He hunts for prey at dead of night
And always gets in the first bite.

John Foster

We're Wolves

Full moon glares,
frost-stars stare,
when we howwwl
and we howwwwl
and we howwwwwl.

Barn owls cry,
bats flit by,
when we howwwl
and we howwwwl
and we howwwwwl.

Heartbeats leap,
goosebumps creep,
when we howwwl
and we howwwwl
and we howwwwwl.

Mike Johnson

Is It Hunting You?

At dead of night, when the moon is full,
it prowls across the moor.
Its fangs are bared, its eyes throb red.
What is it hunting for?

The air is still. Its chilling howls
echo back in time.
Against the moon, its silhouette
sends shivers down your spine.

It's closer now. Don't try to hide,
there's nothing you can do.
It's on its way and you are doomed
if *it* is hunting *you*.

Jane Clarke

Beware the Beastly Boggart

Beware the beastly boggart
With his patched and ragged clothes.
Beware his grubby fingers
And his horrid hairy toes.

Never try to look inside
His dark and dismal pit.
You really wouldn't like it.
No, not one little bit.

The boggart's eating habits
Are messy and quite crude,
For he dribbles when he's drinking
And he slops and slurps his food.

He's very fond of children.
He likes them boiled or fried.
And that's another reason
Why you shouldn't go inside.

So beware the beastly boggart
In his dark and dismal pit.
You really wouldn't like him.
No, not one little bit.

Cynthia Rider

The Bogeyman

In the desolate depths of a perilous place
the bogeyman lurks, with a snarl on his face.
Never dare, never dare to approach his dark lair
for he's waiting . . . just waiting . . . to get you.

He skulks in the shadows, relentless and wild
in his search for a tender, delectable child.
With his steely sharp claws, and his slavering jaws
oh, he's waiting . . . just waiting . . . to get you.

Many have entered his dreary domain
but not even one has been heard from again.
They no doubt made a feast for the butchering beast
and he's waiting . . . just waiting . . . to get you.

In that sulphurous, sunless, and sinister place
he'll crumple your bones in his bogey embrace.
Never never go near if you hold your life dear,
For oh! . . . what'll he do . . . when he gets you!

Jack Prelutsky

The Nokk

Be warned, you little children,
Every son and every daughter,
Who disobey your mums and dads
And play too close to water.

For in every river, stream, and brook,
In lake and pond and lock,
In waterfalls steep and chasms deep,
There lurks the deadly NOKK.

His beard is of a weedy green
His ears like giant oars,
His eyes are the hue of the ocean blue,
And his hands are giant claws.

He sits and waits in his watery cave,
And never makes a noise,
Or silently swims near the surface clear
Looking for girls and boys.

And should he spy a child like you,
Playing near waters deep,
With his click-clack jaws and his snip-snap claws
He'll grab you by the feet.

Then he'll drag you down to his murky depths,
To the watery world of the fish
And on his rock, the deadly NOKK
Will eat his tasty dish.

So be warned, you little children,
And obey your parents, do.
Every son, every daughter, stay away from the water,
Or his next meal might be you!

Gervase Phinn

Bellow

I'm Bellow the ogre,
I rumble and rave.
I'm craggy, volcanic,
My mouth is a cave.
I grumble and thunder
And yammer and fret,
I gobbled a goblin,
My stomach's upset.

I'm Bellow the ogre,
I bluster and boast,
I roasted a troll,
He was perfect on toast.
My manners are grisly,
My temper is hot,
I nibbled a wizard,
My head hurts a lot.

I'm Bellow the ogre,
I smoulder and moan,
I carry a cudgel
Of dragon-tail bone.
I swallowed a giant,
He went down like lead—
Bellow the ogre
Is going to bed.

Jack Prelutsky

Cricklewick Hall

I went to a party
At Cricklewick Hall,
The spooks and the spectres
Were having a ball;

The hostess, a ghostess,
She was, I am sure—
I noticed the moment
She walked through the door.

Colin West

Blocked Passage

The ghost had a bump on his forehead,
It really looked nasty and sore.
He got it when going through the keyhole—
The key had been left in the door . . .

Clive Webster

There Once Was a Ghost Called Paul

There once was a ghost called Paul,
Who went to a fancy-dress ball.
　　To shock all the guests
　　He went quite undressed
But the rest couldn't see him at all.

Anon.

The Skeleton's Invitation

I've nobody to take me to the party.
Can you blame me if I have a little moan?
I'd really like to go, but I'll have to answer No.
I haven't got the guts to go alone.

Kaye Umansky

A Ghostly Party

Old Miss McTavish
sat up in bed
as a ghost glided past.
'Do excuse me,' it said.
'Were you disturbed?
Is the music too loud?
We're having a party.
The usual crowd.
We're going to dance
the skeleton hop,
just voted by ghosts
as the top of the pops.'
The ghosts circled round
with a chorus of groans
waving their arms
and rattling their bones
and old Miss McTavish
lay down in bed
and pulled all the covers
over her head.

Marian Swinger

Skeletons Are Cool

When everyone is sweltering
Beside the swimming pool,
Skeletons get on with life.
Skeletons are cool.

When everyone is feeling limp
Like overcooked spaghetti.
Skeletons get on with life.
Skeletons aren't sweaty.

They always look immaculate.
They always look so neat.
They always dress in bones, you see,
And bones don't overheat.

When temperatures are rocketing,
When dogs begin to drool,
Skeletons get on with life.
Skeletons are cool.

Kaye Umansky

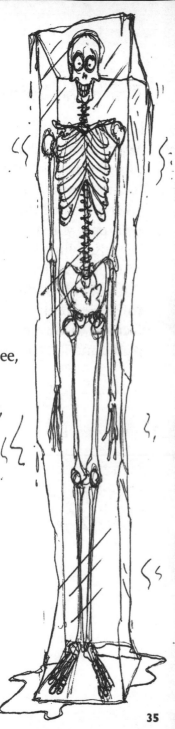

That's the Spirit!

It seems a most rewarding post,
Applying as a trainee ghost
Where one is taught, with moans discreet,
To shake and shimmer in a sheet.
A Mr Dracula's director,
He'll pass you as a spook or spectre.
The discipline is strict, it's true.
You speak when you are spook-en to
Until, come graduation day,
You've frightened everyone away,
A credit to your creepy school,
Well done . . . to every boy and ghoul.

Max Fatchen

Ghoul School Rules

1. Glide, don't flit!

2. Keep your head ON at all times.

3. NO clanking of chains between lessons.

4. No walking through walls. Wait OUTSIDE the classroom.

5. No skeletons to be taken out of cupboards.

6. Line up QUIETLY for the ghost train at the end of the night.

Sue Cowling

Ghost Train

It's a spine-chilling
Tingle-thrilling
Hairy-scary ride.
Yes, the ghost train's the ride
To make you terrified.

Oh, your teeth will start to chatter
At the dismal moans and groans.

And your knees will start to knock
At the grinning skulls and bones.

You will shiver and you'll shake
As the phantoms start to howl.

And you'll quiver and you'll quake
At the bats and screeching owls.

So come and get your tickets
If you want to have a scare,

And get on board the ghost train
If you think you really dare.

It's a horrifying,
Terrifying,
Grim and grisly ride.
Yes, the ghost train's the ride
To make you PETRIFIED!

Cynthia Rider

The Castle Ghost

Here I walk and here I dream,
dust motes twinkling in a beam
of sunlight shafting through the gloom
of this haunted castle room.
Till these dark towers fall I'll stay
dreaming here. Day follows day,
night follows night, but I don't sleep.
Sometimes though, I weep. I weep,
then people shiver and they say,
'The ghost! The ghost has passed this way.'

Marian Swinger

Dave and the Dungeon

Don't go down in the dungeon, Dave,
It's really creepy down there.
The walls are all wet and mossy
And the floor's just dirt—it's all bare.
Fixed in the wall, where they chained people up,
Are these great rusty iron rings
And if you stand there in the silence, Dave,
You'll imagine all kinds of things:
Like the chinking of chains, the rustle of rats,
And the hopeless prisoners' moans;
And it's cold down there and you'll end up, Dave,
Chilled through to your very bones.
Take my advice . . . oh, you're going down.
Well, hang on to that staircase rope.
Don't say I didn't warn you.
Be seeing you soon . . . I hope.

Eric Finney

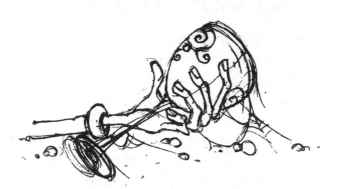

In a Far Land

In a far land
a black mountain broods:
beneath the black mountain
stretch the green woods.

Among the green woods
a white castle soars:
in the white castle
are dark corridors.

The corridors lead
to a black, shut door.
Behind it a Prince
sprawls dead on the floor.

With a cobwebbed cup
by his withered hand,
a Prince lies poisoned
in that far land.

A hobbling old Princess
creeps to the door—
ghost calling ghost
for evermore!

She murmurs her guilt
in sighs and soft moans.
Behind the locked door
the dead Prince groans.

Raymond Wilson

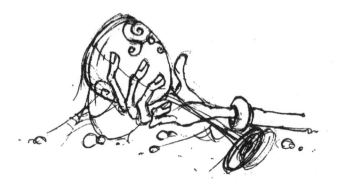

The Old House

The old house stands at the foot of the hill—
Blackened, silent, still.

They say on dark nights
You can hear
The ghost of a laugh,
A cry of fear.

That you can see
Beside the wall
A shadowy figure
Gaunt and tall,
Clutching a bundle
Wrapped in a cloak.

That you can see
The swirling smoke
And hear the crackling
Of the fire
And watch as the flames
Leap higher and higher . . .

The old house stands at the foot of the hill—
Blackened, silent, still.

John Foster

Don't Look Back

Is it just the pattering
Of gently falling leaves,
Or can I hear soft footsteps
Creeping through the trees?

Don't turn round
And don't look back,
The goblin folk are tiptoeing
Along the woodland track.

Is it just the sighing
Of the breeze in the leaves,
Or is there someone whispering
Among the green trees?

Don't turn round
And don't look back,
The goblin folk are scampering
Along the woodland track.

Is it just the sunlight
Sparkling on the leaves,
Or are those watchful eyes
That glisten in the trees?

Don't turn round
And don't look back,
The goblin folk are after you
So RUN along the track!

Cynthia Rider

We're Seven Grubby Goblins

We're seven grubby goblins
You never want to meet,
We fail to wash our faces,
Or clean our filthy feet.
Our hands are always dirty,
We have dishevelled hair,
We dress in shabby leggings
And tattered underwear.

We're seven gruesome goblins,
Our habits are uncouth,
We pull each other's teeth out
Then put back every tooth.
We drink iguana gravy,
We chew polluted prunes,
We dance repugnant dances,
We sing unpleasant tunes.

We're seven grungy goblins,
Determined to displease,
We never blow our noses,
No matter how we sneeze.
We smell like rotten garlic,
We burp around the clock,
This soon should be apparent,
We're moving to your block.

Jack Prelutsky

A Creepy Riddle

My first is in **ghost** and also in **grave**
My second's in **monster** asleep in his cave
My third is in **bogeyman**, **bat**, **blood**, and **bite**
My fourth is in **werewolf** who hunts folk at night
My fifth is in **witches** who cackle and moan
And my last is in **skeleton** and also **tombstone**.

What am I?

Richard Caley

Into the Dark

Let's be daring,
let's be brave,
let's explore
that dark dark cave.

I'll lead the way
beneath the bats
through the cobwebs
past the rats.

Hear our echoes
whisper back,
I'll show the way
into the black.

What's that noise?
We'll have to see.
You'll feel safe
when you follow me.

The cave is filled
with sudden chill,
a moaning, whining
sound so shrill.

It's drawing nearer,
let's all run,
quick as you can . . .
back home to *Mum*!

Tracey Blance

Caliban's Cave

The sand is damp
and cold as stone
when the tide creeps back
from Caliban's Cave.

The rocks are black
as you creep alone
on the dark, damp sand
of Caliban's Cave.

The seagulls sing
and the seashells moan
as they slide in the tide
through Caliban's Cave.

The pebbles ring
like the crack of a bone
as you tiptoe deep
into Caliban's Cave.

The music dies
when the waves have gone
and you stand alone
in Caliban's Cave . . .

*You stand in the heart
of Caliban's Cave . . .*

Judith Nicholls

The Nervous Wreck

Where the sea is as black as octopus ink
a mile below the waves,
the wreck of a sailing ship marks the spot
of a score of sailors' graves.

When storm clouds race and the tide whips foam
the captain's ghost will rise
and walk the cabin and pace the deck,
while the ship gives a shudder and sighs.

Then all at once the skeleton crew
with a rattle and clatter of bones
pull the phantom ropes, raise the phantom mast,
while the ship gives a tremble and groans.

And the conger eel and the squid swim fast
to escape the spectres' wails,
and the deep black water turns colder than ice
while the ship gives a shiver and quails.

Oh, it's not much fun on the ocean floor
for a rusting, nervous wreck
when the ghost of the captain and skeleton crew
take a turn about the deck.

Alison Chisholm

Crazy Smile

Grandad's got a dog,
looks like a crocodile
with its dragon-spiky back
and crazy Dracula-smile.

What's that
your dog's got, Grandad?

What sort of bone
is that?

What's he been burying
in the garden?

Who's been to see you—
they've left their hat.

Joan Poulson

Always

The child at the end of the garden
Holds out her arms to me;
Always I hear her calling
From the shadows beneath the tree.

The child at the end of the garden
Begs me to come and play;
Always her eyes are staring
And her touch is cold as clay.

Penny Dolan

The Swing

The swing sways forward.
The swing sways back,
Forward and back in the sharp frosty air.
Hour after hour, its iron chains creak,
But there's nobody, nobody there.

John Kitching

The Midnight Train to Nowhere

Brambles creep over the platform.
The station is silent and hushed.
The signals are bent and broken.
The tracks are covered in rust.

But people say that on windy nights
When owls are sweeping low,
From deep inside the tunnel
An eerie whistle blows.

And the smell of hot smoke fills the air
And they hear the hiss of steam,
As the Midnight Train to Nowhere
Goes thundering through their dreams.

Cynthia Rider

The Watcher

No one sees me as I sit all alone,
Alone in the old rocking-chair.
No one can see the guitar by my side,
Or the girl with long, golden hair.

No one can see my old, shadowy cat.
No one can see my black rook.
No one can know of the dreams in my head
Or the secrets I hide in my book.

I've been sitting here for hundreds of years,
Watching the fire's bright flames,
And watching as well, though nobody knows,
The world and his wife at their games.

Who is she? You wonder as she sits there alone,
Alone in her old rocking-chair
With her cat and her rook, her book and guitar,
And her girl with the long, golden hair.

John Kitching

The Phantom!

If you want me to come to life
And slowly to appear,

If you want me to leave my grave
And fill your house with fear,

Then wish for me with all your might
And whisper this three times at night!

The Phantom!
The Phantom!
The Phantom!

If you want me to dance and sway
As the light shines from the moon,

If you want me to cry and sing
A distant deathly tune,

Then wish for me with all your might
And whisper this three times at night!

The Phantom!
The Phantom!
The Phantom!

Ian Bland

Ghosts

That's right. Sit down and talk to me.
What do you want to talk about?

Ghosts. You were saying that you believe in them.
Yes, they exist, without a doubt.

What, bony white nightmares that rattle and glow?
No, just spirits that come and go.

I've never heard such a load of rubbish.
Never mind, one day you'll know.

What makes you so sure?

I said:
What makes you so sure?

Hey,
Where did you go?

Kit Wright

Is It True?

'You don't believe in phantoms?
You don't believe I'm true?
That's fine by me,'
Said the little ghost.
'I don't believe in YOU!'

Clare Bevan

Index of Titles and First Lines

(First lines in italic)

Acknowledgements

We are grateful for permission to reproduce the following poems:

Clare Bevan: 'Is It True?' first published in Brian Moses (ed.): *Spectacular Spooks* (Macmillan, 2000), reprinted by permission of the author.

Sue Cowling: 'Ghoul School Rules' first published in Roger Stevens, Sue Cowling, and Jan Dean (eds.): *A Mean Fish Smile* (Macmillan, 2000), reprinted by permission of the author.

Richard Edwards: 'The Alleyway' from *Leopards on Mars* (Viking, 1993), reprinted by permission of the author.

Max Fatchen: 'That's the Spirit!' first published in Jane Coverdale (ed.): *Petrifying Poems* (Omnibus Books, Australia, 1986), reprinted by permission of John Johnson (Authors' Agent) Ltd.

John Foster: 'The Old House', copyright © John Foster 1997, from *Making Waves* (OUP, 1997), 'What's That?', copyright © John Foster 1991 from *Ghost Poems* (OUP, 1991), and 'Count Dracula', copyright © John Foster 2000, first published in Paul Cookson (ed.): *The Works* (Macmillan, 2000), all reprinted by permission of the author.

Mike Harding: 'The Grebs' from *Up the BooAye, Shooting Poo Kakis*, (Savoy Books, 1980), copyright © Mike Harding 1980, reprinted by permission of the author.

Adrian Henri: 'The Lurkers' from *The Phantom Lollipop Lady* (Methuen Children's Books, 1986), copyright © Adrian Henri 1986, reprinted by permission of the author c/o Rogers, Coleridge & White Ltd, 20 Powis Mews, London W11 1JN.

Jack Prelutsky: 'The Bogeyman' from *Nightmares and Other Poems to Trouble Your Sleep* (1976), copyright © Jack Prelutsky 1976, reprinted by permission of the publishers, A & C Black Ltd and HarperCollins Publishers, Inc.; 'Bellow' and 'We're Seven Grubby Goblins' from *Monday's Troll* (Greenwillow Books,1996), copyright © Jack Prelutsky 1996, reprinted by permission of HarperCollins Publishers, Inc.

Kaye Umansky: 'Skeletons Are Cool', 'The Skeleton's Invitation', and 'The Ghost in the Washing Machine' from *Witches in Stitches* (Puffin, 1988), reprinted by permission of the author.

Colin West: 'Cricklewick Hall' from *Long Tales, Short Tales and Tall Tales* (Doubleday, 1995), reprinted by permission of the author.

Raymond Wilson: 'In a Far Land' from *To Be A Ghost* (Viking, 1991), reprinted by permission of G. M. Wilson.

Kit Wright: 'Ghosts' from *Rabbiting On* (Fontana Lions, 1978), reprinted by permission of the author.